I Can't Sleep...

...Because of You.

Thoughts of a Lovestruck Insomniac

I Can't Sleep...

...Because of You.

Thoughts of a Lovestruck Insomniac

Elizabeth Antoinette

Published 2020
Printed in the United States of America
ISBN: 978-0-578-61947-7
Library of Congress Control Number: 2020900026

Edited by Toni Lester & Elizabeth Ann Editing Services

Cover Photography by Daryl Johnson astutelenz.com
Cover Graphic Design by Elizabeth Ross
Final Cover Edits by The BlaQ Knight

An EAR to Write Publishing, Co., and Elizabeth Ann Editing Services are divisions of The Director of Creativity, LLC.

For information, address:
The Director of Creativity, LLC
An EAR to Write Publishing, Co
P.O. Box 31272
Knoxville, TN 37930

thedirectorofcreativity.com

Table of Contents

For: Aunt Mary and Geoffrey

Thank you for nicknaming me *"Superstar."*
I intend to keep making you proud.
I love and miss you all the time.

Miss & love you too Uncle Ro!

An Ode to My Bestfriend, The Pen

The Pen became my Bestfriend
When I found it hard to express myself aloud

It was something about the lump that formed in
my throat that always made it hard to tell someone
an answer I knew was right
Or to express how I was feeling whether happy or
sad
To share my thoughts on anything I felt I couldn't
find the words to verbally say

Kinda like some people find an outlet through
sports or dancing or singing
The Pen was always there to greet me with open
arms
Allowed me to be as open and free as possible
The art of expression became a means of escape

I found that I cleave to my Bestfriend to help me
think clearly and pick apart any turmoil that's
usually bubbling underneath
It's the best way I can get you to understand the
person that is me

And when I'm tongue tied with butterflies in my
stomach and no sentence in sight
I allow my mind to do the talking onto the tablet
and through the Pen I write

A Summary of Sorts

This book is divided into two sections.
The first being the Series of Poems Entitled *I Can't Sleep*.
The second being five of the Ancient Greeks Words for Love.
The Introductory Poems are categorized as sections and the Greek types of Love are to be considered sub-sections.

The 'I CAN'T SLEEP' series

The core of this book is the sentiment of not being able to sleep because of another person, and so being driven to write. With that being said, many of these pieces were written in the wee hours of the morning, though they were not written in any particular order. I may have written 4 of the 6 'I Can't Sleep' poems before I realized they could be used to categorize each section and after that realization was able to divide all the pieces into the sections.

The Greeks Definition of Love

The Ancient Greeks considered Love to be subsidiaries of an overall emotion. Upon researching these words, I realized their importance in understanding what Love is. Any and everyone can love and be loved, but not many understand what it really is. As such, I've included a brief description of the Greeks definitions of Love that I decided to include in the book. These descriptions will also help the Reader understand each piece in each section, and ultimately, the flow of the book.

LUDUS - or playful love
Refers to the early stages of a relationship, including flirting, also, sometimes called the "Honeymoon Stage," however, *Ludus* in conjunction with this book, also refers to harmless enjoyment, silliness and fun between friends

e. antoinette

PHILIA - or deep friendship
Refers to comradery, a love embodied by loyalty between friends. The Greeks definition of *philia* had more to do with a love between brothers who'd withstood battle together, "brotherly love," (i.e. Phila-delphia, the city of brotherly love) *Philia*, in conjunction with this book, is a friendship held in esteem deeper than a romantic relationship

AGAPE- or sacrificial, selfless love
Refers to an extension of love to all people. The Greeks viewed this as the type of love everyone should show to one another. As a Christian, I must include here that *Agape* love is considered the highest expression of Love, a love for mankind, human nature, your fellow brother, the love that Jesus Christ had for all of us, to endure death that we may live a life free from sin. In conjunction with this book, *Agape* is to sacrifice oneself (pride, ego, etc.) for the sake of another

EROS* - or sexual love
Refers to sexual passion and desire. The Greeks didn't necessarily value this type of love positively, in fact, they were assumed to be afraid of it, as it was presumed to be irrational and possessive, which included a loss of control. In conjunction with this book, *Eros* is a sexually infused desire that can become problematic when attempting to separate reality from fantasy

MANIA* - or manic love
Refers to a mixture of lust, possessiveness, and obsession. Not commonly included in mainstreams list of Greek types of love, the Greeks considered this manic love to be a form of madness, or for someone to be "crazed," (i.e., Crazy in Love). In conjunction with this book, *Mania* is the series of emotional highs and lows one can experience in coping with the downfall of a severed relationship

*As the reader will see, *I CAN'T SLEEP PART IV*, hold both *EROS* and *MANIA*, because the Greek's definition of both of those types of loves can be considered one and the same.

PRAGMA - or longstanding love
Refers to mature love, a love coupled with the ability to withstand outside influences to make it last. The Greeks considered this type of love to be filled with patience and tolerance. In conjunction with this book, *Pragma* is love that lasts the tests of time, the love a lot of people can only hope, wish and dream for; and surprisingly, it is love that one may experience at least once a lifetime

PHILAUTIA - or self-love
Refers to love for oneself. The Greeks considered that self-love was important, that with the love of self, one would have the capability to love another/other(s). In conjunction with this book, *Philautia* is the ability to love and cherish oneself, without the influence of another

Enjoy your reading!

e. antoinette

I Can't Sleep Part I

I can't sleep so I'll write
Always up at night
Hearing the loudest quiet
Enticing my rowdy mind
To take shape and create

Seems the longer I'm awake I'm in waiting
For something
For someone
For anything
To happen

But the times I choose are normally when the
world's settled down
And no one is around
That's when I want and desire the most
After day is done and we can no longer see the sun
Or hear the traffic and trains on tracks
When everything is still and all one must do is
relax
That's when the mind is most rowdy
And quiet is the loudest

When I can't sleep, I write

LUDUS
PLAYFUL LOVE
(Fun Between Friends)

ima write you a poem,
about how you put me on sweet tea.
a country girl to the core but raised with northern
tendencies.
no exquisite taste,
never been one thirsty for the finer things,
simplicity'll do just fine for me.

gimme a book to read and a nice big oak with some
shade.
let me rub yo feet under the tree
after i pour you a glass of lemonade
sing to you as we lay in the grass under the stars,
all these pleasantries mixed with your fascination
of my southern drawl.

clinging to your every word,
then cringing with nervous excitement as you
whisper in my ear.
throw me over your shoulder while you run
through the cornfield
and hold me high in the sky once we reach the end
of the lake's pier.

and you'll kiss me while the frogs, and crickets, and
fireflies,
make up all the noises, giving us the only light,
as the darkness enveloping us
makes me forget about the city's night skies.

got me wanting to name my babies after you,
as i sway back and forth to the rhythm of your
voice

and the waters silent songs cries.
but then the moon'll come out and you'll hold me
close
as i look up into your searching eyes.

and i'll giggle as i start sinking into the mud
looking down on our exposed toes.
"where are my shoes?!" i yell, after i steal a kiss on
your cheek
and run back towards the house.

you'll catch up with me, scoop me up
and we'll fall right back under the oak tree.
and i'll lay in your arms and tell you this poem
about how you put me on sweet tea.

Dreadhead

maybe it's your hair
the locks, those locks
with no key to spare
entangled, ardor riled
the strength of my desire
sir Samson
beast of the wild
tell me your secret
make it clear
cause the reality is
it just might be your hair

Oh, How I Wish That It Would Rain

I waited for it to rain all weekend

Don't get me wrong, I love the sun
And the temps at the peak of summer
And the last few weeks of spring
But it's something about waking up to rain on a
Saturday morning
After a long, hard, hot week
Where works been stressful and your lover's been
getting on your nerves
And even though you have a whole checklist of
errands to run
When you wake up to the sound of the rain at your
window
And realize the sun isn't glaring at you
to wake up as it had every morning of the last week
You gotta admit a part of you melts with the drops
that hit the side of the house and rolls off into the
grass
Kinda like you sitting up to push back the curtain
and once seeing the beauty of the gloom looming
the sky due to the rain,
your body sinks back into the pillow, you wrap
back up under the covers
and lay there smiling, staring at the ceiling, taking
advantage of an opportunity
to take a break from the hustle and bustle of life,
and enjoy the rain slowing everything down
I waited every day this weekend to feel those exact
emotions
as the forecast called for rain every other hour
But it never came and I worked my way through
the week and the weekend

Hoping it'd come when I had the most amount of time to waste
and not interrupt the flow of the upcoming week,
as then I'd have the least amount of time to enjoy
the brief sedation of reality
rain brings

April and Florida

You ever stood on the beach with your feet buried
in the sand
Looking across the ocean amazed at the waves
hitting the land
The sun beating your brow and the wind combing
your hair
You stretch your arms out wide just to hug the
passing air
And suddenly there's a sprinkle of rain that hits
your face
Surprisingly enough it's abrupt entry leaves no
room for escape
So you stand and bask in what becomes rain
Hair wet and tangled, bodies all around you
scattering
Trying to find shelter, seeking dryness wondering
from where it even came
After a few moments, the sun comes out back from
behind the clouds
And the rain lightens to none, prompting the
return of the crowds
And the chill the rain brought returns back a slight
feeling of comfort
A little warmth, along with a few breezes coming
from the direction of the ocean
And you've stood there to experience it all
Watching the earth play with the temperatures
Like a child whose found the thermostat settings
on the wall
Watching the ocean go from peaceful to riled in a
matter of minutes
And the sky's open and close, like the doors leading
into a business

If you don't find delight in this most beautiful
Floridian weather
As everything is most perfectly calm before a
storm
Then you couldn't comprehend the joy of the
seasons change from winter to spring in April
When one day even though the sun is beaming
upon you the temps are close to freezing
And the next day it's hot enough to choke your
breathing
But then there's a week of perfect days
With flowers abloom and the sky's always inviting
And those same nights are filled with
thunderstorms that leave by dawn
Having the next day feeling not too warm but not
too cold, almost enticing
Makes you want to stay outside and make others
believers of the curse that is Spring Fever
But if you can't understand the joy that is the
month of April
Surely you can't love her cousin Florida
You'd simply be unable
You see the two are almost identical
One's annual appearance and the other's daily
occurrence
Makes them the greatest of their separate
categories
But relative in perfection, in other words

I Can't Sleep Part II

I can't sleep
.... And all I can think about is you.

When did this happen and why
Not a fan of vulnerability
I prefer logic and things seen with the naked eye
Emotions and feelings can be so overwhelming

Especially when you find yourself up writing
All because you're dwelling
On what if's and could be's
In the middle of the night
And for once looking for something to disturb the peace
That is the quiet
that's driven your mind so deep...
...Into thought
And you're only surrounded by things that you've bought

Cause your guard is up too high to allow anyone in
So, there you lie stuck with the feelings brewing within
Both desiring and despising what could be considered comfort from another
Not able to sleep because you're too stubborn to admit that you love him

I can't sleep...

Because of you.

PHILIA
DEEP FRIENDSHIP
(A Friendship Deeper than Romance)

Twin Flame

You're like my subconscious, but out loud
I usually know exactly what I'm thinking or feeling
And even often know the solution to problems
But like all humans, sometimes we can get caught
up in a swirl of over thought
And that's where you come in for me
The truth that I know deep down inside
But sometimes need a kick to tap into
You're like my subconscious, but out loud
And I don't know what I'd do without you

We belonged to each other for so long
This new feeling is so wrong
I'm used to leaving
And you're used to coming
Even with words unspoken
We could always come back
Now the circle is broken
I was so stupid
I loved you so much
You got what you wanted
Here I am missing your touch
When you probably never think of me
I gave you all of me...
And now she has all of you
Wish I could see that view
Feel how that feels and tastes how that tastes
Instead, I'm just left with the reminder of a waste
of time and love and money and us
and it never meant anything to you
fuck was an us?
It was you it was me
And now it's just me
And it's her and it's you
The we I wanted to be
And my tears and my pain
Forever unsustained
And not even able to tell my best friend I miss him.
What a shame.

I'm a Protector

if I feel the need to let you be, that means I'm
confident that you're strong enough to handle
yourself

my heart is closed so all I can do is
protect you to show I care
I may not say it or mention it
but I'm watching and monitoring
you say I hate you I'm done with it
but you stay cause you fuck with me
and you know I'm just struggling
to show the love that's within me
so I hope you'll forgive me
of the times I ain't listening
but I'm really attentive
just can't help the insensitive
the shit that lives in me
cause the last time I showed sympathy
I wound up this empty

if we became one would that make you forget
everything?
would conquering as many as you can
no longer matter as ensuring?
could us change your mindset on what
you think of longevity?
could our friendship be the defining
factor of love and prosperity?
i can see it but can you?

i hope and pray for us to be just two
but i guess it's taking longer for you
to admit it
i want so much for us and dream of the
day it is
you proclaiming yourself as hers and
me as his
not to be confused with lust we've
reached a turning point
i love you as a friend but i'm ready to
love with the sole purpose of us
becoming joint

I Want Them All to Myself

I miss **him**
Don't know how I'd live without **him**
Wish **he'd** come back
Want to make **him** more than **he** realizes
And I want them all to myself

Never wanted to be a player, never saw myself this
way
But the fact of the matter is I got love for all my
"**friends**"
A gift and a curse, this friendship matter,
cause now I'm stuck

So, I drown myself in work cause I have more
control over it than love
I know I can't keep running from it
and one day it'll eventually catch up with me
but my comfortable seldom allows change
which has deemed itself worthless
as all my former "**friends**" turned lovers and vice
versa
are now just as stuck as me when it comes to me

Double Consciousness

THE DREAM

Wonder if he feels the same
Like me does he imagine me screaming his name
I wonder if he dreams the dreams
if he thinks the things,
the same very things
the things that mean the most
when I speak of him I boast
I smile a smile, the smile unseen
for time has passed since the smile saw a scene
wonder does he smile the smile, the same very
smile
the one that makes my heart gleam
could it be the same very things I say when I'm
away
He says the same in his own very special way
does he wonder if and wonder when
wonder the time we end as friends and begin again
but this time to transcend
the time when these thoughts were only when
and only if
but would we drift
would we regret the if
regret the when
regret the time we end as friends
or should we depress the wonder
forget the dream
and rather me not scream his name
should we remain
wonder does he think the same...

THE REALITY

That's just my wondering my brain
He probably doesn't think a thing
Neither does he feel a thing
Nothing's the same
Nothing I thought ever became
A thought to say the same
Of course it's never crossed his mind
He's never called me his mine
He's never thought a thing of this matter
His mind has never dreamed
Never saw the things I seen
Of us
Of we
We belong
But of course he just plays along
A friend he knows he is that and that alone
He's never thought these things
Not of me
Never realized it's to me he clings
Just a friend is all it means
Though to me it does not seem
So clear through smoke screens
The truth revealed of those things
But I'll accept these things he does not see
And leave the dreams
the wonder
to me.

Prince Charming

I met Prince Charming once
And he was nothing like what I imagined...

When we first met we hated each other's guts
But he swears he was told otherwise
That his friends told him on him I had a crush
How untrue and false of a statement
I had my eyes on what I'd consider my type, so he's
indeed mistaken
Of the recollection that I was ever interested
But when we did become friends there was no
denying the chemistry
It came like a rushing wind that overpowered me
From strangers into confidantes the bond was
astounding
And we argued and fought like sisters and brothers
From the outside looking in people called it lovey-
dovey
He wasn't much of a looker to me but he carried
himself with such high standards
Whenever I was with him I wanted to match his
fly and mind my manners
And full of stubbornness and unnecessary rebellion
Outside of my mother, he was the only one that
could tame my inner hellion
The one that popped out when things didn't go my
way
He'd always know how to make things better,
always knew just what to say
He had a way of taking control without you
realizing it, but I never minded with him
It felt good to be able to be vulnerable, his very
aura enlightened my day

I look back now and realized he spoiled me, but not
with material things, only,
But compassion and warmth endearing
The kind that makes you drive for hours on end in
the snow on freezing roads
On a trip that usually takes 3
And the way he took care of me was something I
couldn't have possibly ever dreamed of, but I never
showed my awe
I always felt like the belle of the ball when I looked
in his eyes and he'd smile back,
Making me wonder when he looked at me what he
saw
Now, to some, he was a goofball, and too much to
handle for others,
But one of the smartest men I'd ever met
Not quick to brag on himself, a young mogul in the
making, but probably one of the countriest
bumpkins you'll ever meet, I bet
And we'd laugh for hours on end or sometimes just
sit in silence
But both were always the most awesome
experiences I've ever had
The most peaceful I'd ever felt
His presence alone was my solace
Unfortunately, a fire didn't burn within me initially
Years had gone by before I can honestly say I felt
anything
And in all the time that had passed on before, I
knew because of this he wasn't my Prince
Charming
Even though he'd open doors, and pay for meals,
and sometimes even rescued me

From the bummy guys I called myself in love with,
he'd go out of his way to try and make them jealous
of him and afraid to lose me
And not once did I stop to think maybe I should
give him a chance
He'd mention it to me but I'd mastered the little
song and dance
Of being just friends and not feeling the same way
Even when he'd find ways to help make my dreams
come true with any hesitance or questions asked
And yet I didn't even look his way

Til one night I opened my eyes and realized just
because he didn't fit my definition of who my
Prince Charming should be,
He was indeed not a Prince, but instead exactly
what I needed
And to this thought I took heed,
The man that brings the Queen out of you,
is the man who deserves to be your King.

You Showed Me Love

I can't get the words out when it comes to you
I can't fix my mouth to utter the truth
The fact that I even feel the way I do
It's hard to admit it,
I love you
And it's sort of pathetic

I mean why didn't I see it when you first told me
Why couldn't I feel the same way with all the ways
you showed me
Why am I just now knowing it
When you've finally let go of it

And I laugh cause it's too late
You were right there all along and I just kept
running away
Stuck in my head of how I wanted things to be
Not realizing that you were always the best for me

Focusing on the past and trying to rewrite the
future
All the while finding comfort in your unconditional
love
Picking me up and dusting me off out of my love
drunken stupor

And me never acknowledging that you were
teaching me real love
That even if I can't have you I'll always love you
and be there for you
The Bodyguard type Love

And though it breaks my heart that things will
never be the same
I'll be sure never to run from a love like yours
again
Even if it comes packaged as a best friend

I Can't Sleep Part III

I can't sleep and I wish you were up with me

Did you know you were my sunshine on a cloudy
day?

I love you for your wisdom
And your patience with me
I love your understanding
How you're so conscious of me
I love how even when I'm wrong
You always find the right in me
I love the way you teach me
And handle me so delicately

I love how you pay attention to the smallest details
And remember each and every one when it pertains
to me
I wish there were more of you so everyone could
experience this type of admiration
But more than anything I wish you were mine
So I wouldn't have to hide all this gratification

AGAPE
SACRIFICIAL
(A Love for someone greater than oneself)

What is Love?
But an intensified illusion
An engorged emotion
Causing us to crash right into strangers
Who otherwise would've never served us any
purpose
Turning us into the greatest of friends or the
deepest of lovers
And ultimately changing our lives forever.

I can't talk to you cause I feel like everything's
gonna pour out

I want to tell you how grateful I am to have you in
my life
How I'm so glad you help my dreams come true
And I wanna ask you how I can help you reach
yours?

I want to tell you how my heart aches to be closer
to you whenever we're apart
How I'm so happy whenever we're near
And I wanna ask you, do you feel the same?

I want to tell you that you're always on my mind
every second and minute of the day
How I'm so excited to simply daydream of past,
present, and future with you
And I wanna ask you, do you ever dream of me
too?

I want to love you and hug you and kiss you and
hold you...
but I have to stop myself from getting so caught
up.

And I wish you'd show me a sign that it's okay for
me to feel like this.

Here I go again
Obsessing over something that may never happen
Dreaming about something I truly want but am
afraid to accomplish
I mean how can deciding to love be looked at as
something so huge
Even though it really is as important as eating
Love can be food
It can be inspiration and encouragement
The help one needs just to make a right decision
And you give me all of that
You complete my vision
But I'm too afraid to fall in love
Too afraid to say how I feel
Afraid to admit these feelings may be the real deal
So I'm fighting myself and forcing myself to leave
it alone
To stay in my comfort zone
Not stressed or worried or anxious
Not thinking about an us
Just doing me and being free
Seems the best way to be
So why am I obsessing over something that may
never happen
Maybe because I really do want it, but only
secretly

The odds are against us
The critics say we can't be in love
They say a love like ours is bound to end
But if they only knew in you I've found a lover and
best friend
And if it took my whole life
Every day I'd want to see you win

The signs say we're not compatible
That a love like ours takes too much work
And the willpower we don't have
But if only they could see how you light up when
you see me
And that you'd give up everything just for me

So it doesn't matter what he thinks or she thinks
Or what they say about us
I just know I wanna be with you
And I don't care
They just want a love like ours

Why Do You Love Me?

I'm not the prettiest
I'm not the richest
So why do you love me so
Not the slimmest
Not the thickest
So why do you adore me so
I'm not the nicest
Surely not the sweetest
So why do you crave me so
I'm not the flyest
Or the most stylish
So why do you want me so

Is it because I'm quirky and goofy
And sarcastic and ruthless
Does my passion match yours
Do you see your suave' in my smoothness
Did my intelligence win you over
Or was it my smile
What captured your heart?
What made you go the extra mile?

Tell me, I'm listening
What are all the things that made you choose me?
And if you want my answer to the same
I love you because you first loved me.

Beautiful Smile

Please don't look at me
I don't want to be seen
Because I don't know what you see
Is it the person in the mirror looking back at me
Or is it a version you've picked of potentiality
Can you see the flaws that are so obvious to me
The pain behind the smile that shines so brightly
The tears in my eyes that have found shelter in the
corners so tightly
What is it that makes you stare
And grin inquisitively
And when I catch you, makes your smile widen the
Grinchestly

I asked of him these things and this is what he said
to me

I see a broken heart afraid to love again
And a guard up so high no one can get in
I see a daughter, a sister, and to many a best friend
Someone who's always giving but never receiving
the helping hand
Yet steadfast and earnest in well-doing
I see a strong and loyal woman
Who'd rather have an opportunity for vulnerability
but has had to follow a path of sensibility that
keeps her feet on the ground with little room for
naivety
And I stare because you've found comfort in a
scowl
And I wish you saw what I saw
That you're most beautiful when you smile

e. antoinette

Catch Me If You Can

I'm good at running away
I never much learned quite how to stay

I mean I know how to pretend like I'll stay put
But I've never conquered silencing the need to go
afoot

There's an urge within me that I can't contain
And it's rearing its ugly head to my disdain

There's an aching in my chest on down to my feet
And I just need to know, if I follow it will you
come catch me?

I just wanna be in your presence
Sometimes I don't have anything to say
But I wanna revel in your existence
Admire you face to face
And crave you from a distance
And in those seldom instances
Where I can sense the same from you
I wish you'd say aloud that you're thinking it too

I'd rather have your presence than your voice
As most times the drain of the day
Leaves me wanting to find solace in silence
And comfort in your arms.

I Can't Sleep Part IV

I can't sleep...
Cause I miss you.

I miss us.
The fighting, the fussing,
Making up, discussing
All the things we'd try to do differently
Only words, no actions
Confrontations, no sympathy

But when things were good
They were fantastic
Best friends and lovers
Finding my counterpart
Thinking love I'd finally mastered

But things never seemed quite right
A couple of days, a couple of nights
And then back at square one
Both too stubborn to see the light
That maybe we could've made it
If either of us was willing to sacrifice

And the love we made
Made it harder to give it up
As our emotions were caught up in the depth of
our lusts
But its perfect mixture made our connection good
enough

And I can't help but think about it
Every so often
How your eyes were the brightest

And your lips were the softest
How you'd say you wanted to do the same if I
asked to kiss you
And how fast you'd respond if I text you
I miss you
But I can't and I won't
Cause this cycle never ends
So, I'll fight my sleep with thoughts of you
And leave what could've been our future
In my dreams instead

EROS
SEXUALITY
(Sexually infused desire)

Burn Baby

There's an ache in the pit of my stomach
A sensation similar to the feeling of hunger
A yearning of some sort
An impression marked on me
A pulling, a tugging
A stirring of fire, growing and burning
And it constantly rises with every step and every
day awakened
A feeling, an arousal of emotions
Soul clenching and breathtaking

And it only gets stronger

With every smile from you
I no longer feel weakness
Every time you listen to me
My guard comes down easier
Whenever I hear from you
My heart beats faster
With every minute we share
Me as the student and you as the master

Your love for me
overpowers my anxiety
that it's impossible to ever experience a love so
deep
It has any influence over your anatomy

And so the ember keeps growing
And I'm barely able to contain it
Your influence on me showing
And the state of ecstasy I'm in is ever flaming

e. antoinette

I have enough R&B for the both of us
Enough rhythm and blues, enough soul and
smooth
You provide the rough, the rock, the roll, the hard
and the cool
Then meet me in the middle
And we'll make the music of lovers
More symphonic than the originators
And use instruments unheard of
Orchestra conductors can't tame
You can be the beat and I'll provide the lyrics
And make a song so sweet we can't name it
Let's mix our substances like mad chemists
And when we're done, we'll sit back and smirk over
the soundwaves
And I'll remind you that I told you my R&B was
enough for the both of us

round and round

I keep replying to your texts, you keep answering
my calls...

these nothing ass conversations...just give me this
momentary relief.

like an avid cigarette smoker who wants to quit so
damn bad but needs a puff every so often,
like a coke feign who wants to quit cold turkey but
gets that unscratchable itch every now and then,
just needing a little feel of the needle to the skin,
how I badly want to never think of you or have
ever even known you,
I was introduced to a drug that engulfed my whole
being,
the smell of it, the taste of it, the satisfaction...
I thought I was dreaming.

You became my addiction.

the beginning of any fixation is always the most
exciting,
but the reality was and still is most addictions just
become bad habits to break,
no matter how enticing,

so, I keep replying to your texts and you keep
answering my calls...

The Way We Love

I love to love you
I'm addicted to that love
You keep dangling it
Right above me
And then pulling it back
Knowing I won't leave
I look forward to that love
I even dream about it
I'm never truly satisfied until
I receive some of that love
Never enjoy it too much
Cause I know the real meaning
Why I love the way you love
Is because you and I know
That the feeling is not of love
But of lust
For we don't have the time to claim
We know real love

e. antoinette

Sour Patch Kids

I knew at first glance you were no good for me
I tried to stay away
But resistance couldn't break the chemistry

How I wish I'd never looked upon your face
But the passion I feel towards you
Could never be replaced

Like cat and mouse this game we play
You're the sun and I'm the moon
But we can't seem to separate the night from day
And in the darkness is where we find each other
From the beginning, it was our favorite place
But when we're not there
The same compassion and care we seem to
misplace

I'm always anxious to leave
And you always take me back
You always ask for more
And I give you everything, but more from you I
seem to lack

You were never any good for me
Nor me for you
But our bodies loved each other
And made us think we did too

I can never escape the thoughts that
We had the potential to be great
Karma dealt us both hands too good not to play
And neither of us won the game of love in any way
Why is it always so hard for us to stay away

e. antoinette   85

to love & lust...to love in lust... to lust in love

love & lust

wanna stay up all night, wrapped up, lying in your
arms
just watching the moon, and the stars,
til the sun decides to return
eyes red with anger, but a heart too filled to leave
holding on to you but dying inside
why'd you make it so hard to breath
the moon lit up and peeking through the window
at our bodies intertwined
darkness drowning the realities between us
exempting what could be of yours and mine
with every gasp and moan, both finger
tips and toes align with the stars
every scratch and clinging moment
doing absolutely nothing to take place of the
internal scars
eyes red with anger but a heart too filled to leave
defined by an amorous passion
recurring feelings of lust surpassing the truth of
your deceit

It Just FEELS Right

skin. sweat. passion.
I swear I float when I leave your side
sighs. moans. delight.
I smile simply thinking of the ecstasy you provide
comfort. relief. perfection.
laying with you just feels so right
dreams. hopes. wishes.
thoughts of you and I fill my head every night
unsure. hesitant. reluctant.
they say if it seems too good to be true
that indeed may be the case
smiles. laughs. blushing.
the happiness that flashes across my face
you. me. us.
we both have pasts whose thoughts about
are the least bit favorable
tomorrow. next month. next year.
only time will tell if to continue we will be capable
always. forever. eternity.
in these words, I don't believe
now. today. the present.
I'll enjoy till the day you decide to up and leave

She don't wanna be saved

I never needed you to save me from me
Let me be a wreck and bask in the debris
I don't need you to make the decision that you and
I together may not be right
Let me figure it out and in the meanwhile enjoy
your presence helping me sleep at night

Let me want you
Let me need you
Let me breathe you
Let me love you
Let me hold you
As much I'd like

And if you're the worst thing that could ever
happen to me
Let me fall flat on my face
I promise I can get back up on my own
It's nothing new
As you can see, I'm back in the race

So right now
Be the music, the rhythm, the tune, to all my songs
And let me be, leave me free
To love you just as much as I'd like
Trust I don't need saving
These patterns of love are the stories of my life

.

MANIA
HIGHS AND LOWS
(Crazy in Love...literally)

It's Always Worse When They're Still Living

I'm forced to devour all my emotions...

But as any meal ravished, they never properly
digest.

I'm left with a stomachache and no Pepto Bismol
For there is no medicine created for such an ache
How, then, do I cope with the pain
At the pit of my stomach
I heard it was unhealthy,
Cancerous even...
I pray it doesn't become an ulcer.
Years of buildup, you'd think
It'd happened by now, you know
Some sort of release...
But no, each time only
Adds more gunk to the pile
No enzymes to break it all down
Just stuck living with all these emotions
That have no place to go.

every time

I walk in the same direction
at the same time of day
that place, the last place, I saw you there
I retrace my steps simply to try and see your face
again
Each time I walk into your favorite location
I can't help but watch my back in case
you surprise me with your presence

It didn't use to be like this
I didn't have to guess where I'd run into you
You used to tell me
Something happened
Now I wait to hear from you
I wait for our spontaneous meetings
For those are the only times I'm able to
Quench my thirst that is you

What Was I Supposed to Do?!

Stay sad for the rest of my life
Keep mourning you like you dead when
you 400 miles away
Wait for you to come back...

You tell me, what did you want me to do?
Hold on when all you did was push me away
Keep looking at my phone waiting for the
text or the call that never came
Allow you to flaunt the strength
they boosted you up to have
Hide my true my feelings when all I wanted
was the person I fell in love with to reemerge?
Is that what you wanted me to do?

Well hell, I couldn't.

Who do you think you are, you just gonna stroll
right back in like nothing ever happened? hmm?
Who do you think you are, ima welcome you
back with open arms? HMM?!

You're so afraid to miss out on what you
think everybody's doing and too dumb
to realize you're missing out on something
everybody's not entitled to have

But I do wanna let you know This,
I did TRY to wait...
you just took too long.

karma

I wish you the best
I'm lying
I hope you fall on a knife
and lie there dying
then I'll be laughing
standing over you
like you do me, just laughing
I love you so much
I'm lying
I hope you shoot yourself in the head
and lie there dying
then I'll be there looking
right into your face
like you do me, just looking
I smile when I think of you
I'm lying
I hope you rot in hell
and spend eternity falling and dying
and I'll be there sipping my water and watching
like you do me, just watching
I wish you all the happiness
I'm lying
I hope you experience everything I did
and spend your nights crying
and I'll just keep smiling
grinning from ear to ear
like you do me, just smiling
I hope you find true love
I'm lying
I hope you get your heart broken into a thousand
pieces
and spend every waking day just dying
and it won't matter to me

cause I'll keep living like it never happened
like you did me...like it never happened.

Now That You're Back

I don't wanna relive all that shit
ain't no stability in it
it's like I want it but don't
you think I need you and I don't
or is it you with the needing
cause I'm done with believing
the shit you said was unreal to me
and though I forgive you
I'm more relieved
to have no worries and keep on just doing me
I'm nowhere near being mean
I just can't see no more you and me

Two Can't Play That Game

Confused isn't the word cause I know what I'm
doing
It's hard separating this game from my emotions
Hell, I'm only human

I've dealt with this before
So, nothing surprises me
Not even your cutesy little lines
About how much you adore me

It would seem I could easily refrain from all
communication
But my curiosity won't let me resist,
Your presence alone is tempting provocation

Your touch, those lips, those eyes, that...
The very essence of you...
But too much is enough to make any girl sick...

So charming yet frustrating
So egotistical and arrogant
Yet sweet and titillating

Unsure of what to do with you this time around
Keep you and try again
Or love you and leave you
Both choices cleverly profound

The lover in me wants to try again
But the hurt in me says diss him like he did you
Fuck him over like you were the man
And then act as if you had no clue

So, I'll try and take each day as it comes
Avoiding what the ultimate decision will and
should be
It's just such a shame that even with all this
thinking and
Optimism about the whole situation
You're sure to be the death of me
When will I ever learn?
Playas don't change
They only come back to claim what they
Feel they lost out on
But never really earned
And there are never any winners in unrequited
love
For two can never really play that game

I Know It Doesn't Matter

I didn't call back to see if it mattered
I see it didn't
Just like I expected
But I'm expecting too much
And I know you're not mine
But I don't think you understand
You're the closest thing I have to comfort
If I could take you and put you in another person
Trust me you wouldn't hear from me
But your attention is what I crave
It's what I desire
And what I've become accustomed to
There's nothing you can do that'd make me leave
your side
Cause you're not mine I can pretend
I don't care and feign that emotion till it manifests
Deep down I wish you'd consider the possibilities
You're so full of nonchalance and this I love and
despise
Because we match
Like two peas in a pod
But I'm crazy for these thoughts and that I can
admit
So I keep em to myself
and every time I test you to see if it really matters
I keep proving myself right

Starry Eyed

I've always liked to gaze at a night sky
The beauty of nature
The reality that there's something greater
Something undeniably real ruling
The skies intrigue me

One night the moon shared space with me in my
room
And I shoved him to wake up and take a look with
me
He grunted out of his sleep and a huff
I said, "Look! It's staring back at us!"
He muscled up a head nod and rolled back over
And at that moment, I knew we'd never grow any
closer

That was years ago
I tried to share the moon and the stars with him
For some reason it was taken as a joke

Though I still feel the same as I did then
As if you'd ever notice
I keep my fascinations to myself

What Day Is This?

Night falls, I cry
In the day, I smile
Night falls again, I remember
Tomorrow, I forget

Thursday, I thought of you
Friday night, I drank away all the memories
Saturday, I sin
Sunday, I pray

Last month, the same old story
Next month, we meet again

Yesterday, I loved you
Tonight...I still do

I Hate You
I Hate thinking about You
I Hate the fact you don't remember Me
I Hate that I have to move on without
understanding
I Hate you turned out to be everything you claimed
not to be
I Hate that You're blind and naive to the shit
around You
I Hate things that remind me of You
I Hate that I don't really know how I feel about
You
I Hate that You're still a factor
I Hate how much I have to disguise how I feel
I Hate how much You changed Me
I Hate You with almost the same passion I loved
You with
I really Hate You

slow dance

I stood there, in the middle of my room and slow
danced to Al Green's, *Simply Beautiful*...with his
shirt...which had long lost the scent of him, but
with tears in my eyes tried to reenact that scene...a
scene I remembered...how could it have meant
nothing...nothing at all to him...I used to slow
dance all the time...previously...with him, but not
him, him as in, the love of my life...I remember
during the breakup, I asked him, "please would you
not share the slow dance with anyone else...can I at
least have that?"...he laughed. guess that was a
no...you danced with me...when I hadn't felt that in
years...the urge to slow dance...you awakened that
in me...and it didn't matter as much until that
night...the night I danced with your shirt, to the
song we'd slow danced to months ago, together, Al
Green's, *Simply Beautiful*, but that night, alone,
dancing with your shirt, trying to recall your scent,
every word he sang had a new meaning...

if i gave you my love
i tell you what i'd do
i'd expect a whole lot of love out of you
you gotta be good to me, i'm gonna be good to you
there's a whole lot of thangs you and i could do

simply beautiful

what about the way you love me and the way you squeeze me
simply beautiful
when you get right down to it
when you needed me i was right there
beside you girl, i care and baby

sometimes when you're feeling low
all you got to do is call me
simply beautiful
                          -Al Green

I Can't Remember

Don't tell anyone but sometimes I sit and think of
you
On these mind trips, I try my hardest to remember
the good times
Scenes flash like pictures falling out of a photo
album
As if I'm floating above those exact moments
I look down on us, looking at each other,
Smiling at each other, loving each other, and I
smile...

With the blink of an eye, I'm back to reality
And it's hard to even imagine that any of those
things ever happened
The tears that filled my eyes for months are even
dried up
I try my best to recapture any bit of emotion left
but there's no luck
I attempt to question what went wrong but all I
get is static
As if 'us' were merely a dream
The good or the bad, I just can't seem to remember

The ring is in the box, the bear is on my bed
The shoes line the closet floor as my others do
I still wear the jacket...
But these material things have all lost the
sentiment they once held...
But what happened to my key?

A part of me wants to hold on to what I knew of
you

And the other part convinces me that I never really
did
Time won't sit still long enough to even let me
figure out my own thoughts
So, I try my best to remember everything, but I
just can't

.... can you?

I feel like I'm in a dream world
Having to live without you
I never realized how much you kept me grounded
Until one day I looked up and to my amazement
saw that nothing really seems the same
It's like my reality is not quite that
Like I'm living a life outside of what's really going
on
Because I don't have you
And I wonder if you feel the same

I can't think of anyone to share my thoughts with
No one who will understand me quite like you did
No one to sit in silence with
Or debate with or dream with
And I can't believe it's taken me this long to realize
that I actually miss you

I was so angry at you that I decided I was done
And what's funny is you didn't come after me
...and you still haven't
Which is the reason I think I was able to stay mad
for so long
But now I'm like where is my piece of sanity,
Which is you

Through laughter, tears, excitement, and gloom
We were always there for each other
But now that we're apart I feel like I'm living life
through a looking glass
Waiting on someone to give me the okay to step
outside
And I realize that person used to be you

I miss you.

e. antoinette   119

I look for your face everywhere I go
I yearn for your scent that I can't smell anymore
My heart still quickens whenever you're near
And you forgetting me is my biggest fear

You're a part of my innocence
A part of my past I can never get back
And though I'll love you forever and cherish every
memory
At the same time, I wish I could get rid of you
And rid myself of the experience of what a real love
could be
Before the reality that love isn't all that it's made
out to be was revealed to me
I want so badly to go back in time and press
rewind and then freeze
And live in the moments that I thought would last
forever
But since I can't
I wish I could get rid of you
And the memory of the innocence you stole from
me

Get out of my dreams
You're haunting me

Mask Off

I used to think you were so perfect and had it all
together
I used to think you could do no wrong
Disillusioned and blind to the reality of the you I
wanted to be a part of
This concept of perfection
But I only wanted a portion
Not all of it in its entirety
And now that I've gotten a taste of it
It's not all that it's been cracked up to be
You're just like me and everyone else around us
But able to put on a façade better than the norm
You found comfort in playing pretend
And hiding behind an appearance that had been
well put together
And now that the mask is off, I don't know if I
want to stay put
And deal with the imperfection that is you
And accept the similar flaws I thought you had the
remedies to
And help you grow into the person you have yet to
become
That I thought you already were
I was impressed by something that didn't even
exist
And now that the fantasy has worn off
I'd feel guilty to leave you as naked as you are
Because I chose to strip you down to nothing

Nothing Else to Write About

I used to think I Needed you
Not wanted but Needed
That it was a Necessity that you knew every little
detail
To spill every little bean
To sow every little seed
Of ups and downs, smiles and frowns
Something somewhere deep inside felt an urge to
keep you in the loop
And I guess you felt the same way too
And I wonder if all who've experienced their first
love early on, only to lose them
Have a small desire to find a way to stay in each
other's lives even when the passion is long gone
There were many moments I searched within to
figure if I even felt the same
But the puppy love had turned familial and I
scoffed at any thought of reconciliation
Yet, somehow the thought of you always seems to
resurface
I guess there will always be a bit of a longing to
redo or even outdo the beauty of that kind of love
And so, the purity of what was once shared always
give me enough umph! to create
And even though we don't speak any longer, and I
have no wish to reach out
I always use you as a muse when I have nothing
else to write about

I Can't Sleep Part V

I can't sleep

And I can't take this song off repeat

Everything about it reminds me of you and me
How it used to be
How love was never-ending
Our souls forever blending
First lovers and loves
The perfect tale

And I'm reminiscing

I loved to love you
I loved to smell you
To be around you
To touch and feel you
Much deeper than the physical
I could bare my being
And our kindred hearts shared the same beating
There was no you without me
No me without you
Only us completing
Each other in time and space
And the passion showed on both our faces

Maybe it was the purity of a first love
That made things blissful
Each moment together
Our love grew stronger, our bond grew tighter
Amorously obsessive

I was yours and you were mine

A love like ours comes once in a lifetime

And this song just keeps reminding me
So, I can't take it off repeat

All the words resounding in my heart
Keep me from falling asleep

PRAGMA
LONGSTANDING LOVE
(A Love that Stands the Tests of Time)

Forever Yours

The tallest mountain couldn't stand in my way
Lightning could strike knocking out all power and
your smile would still brighten my day

An earthquake meant to separate us
couldn't keep me from you

A tornado's fury could blow me away
but the strongest of winds couldn't keep me from
coming back to you

Hail could fall from the heavens
destroying everything in its path
But only the tests of time will be proof
in how long we last

No seemingly insurmountable obstacle
will ever be more than just that
If for you on my death bed
I'd allow that line to go flat

All the words in the world could never
describe exactly how I feel
I could write a thousand poems, a million letters
and none of them would say everything and that's
real

I'd give my all at any given moment or time
If I were the sun and you were the moon, my
illumination I'd share just so you could shine

If strength were all I had to show
I'd knock out the strongest of boxers with just one
blow

Even after all the romance, flowers, and gifts are
no more exciting
My love won't be unending and my heart forever
inviting
Tests and trials, both guarantees in life
Won't be my exit, because giving up isn't an option
and you're definitely worth the fight

When unexpected conditions show up in your
forecast, trust I can weather the storm
I'll be that human comfort, that guide,
that strength when you're weak and worn

Through hardships, through success,
championships and even closed doors
No matter the circumstances or situation, I'm
down, willing and ready for whatever, but most
importantly, forever yours.

First Love, Forever Friends

I have never loved anyone the way I loved you
I was so into you I used to think you could feel
when I wanted you without me having to call your
name
I trusted you with my whole life
and didn't doubt a word that came out of your
mouth
I would have died for you to show the depths of my
love
I entrusted you with my very essence
because I knew you loved me the way I loved you
and you would never betray me
I believed in every wish, hope or dream you had
and was ready with a plan just for whatever you'd
ask
I wanted to serve and satisfy you in any and every
capacity
And if there was ever a time your satisfaction
might not have been the most comfortable
the love I had for you overshadowed any hesitance
I loved you and you loved me
You went out of your way to do whatever I asked
of you
You catered to me as if I was your Queen
You poured your love on me in ways I never
dreamed
Showing vulnerability I'd never witnessed in a man
And always being ready to support and protect me
no matter the cost

This was our love.
The most vulnerable, compromising, sacrificial, but
ardor filled state I'd ever been in.

How could I possibly ever love this way again?
And probably why you, my first love, and I, your
first love, will forever be friends.

I used to think I knew what Love was
And I'm probably still off just a little bit
But if it looks anything like you? Like us?
I think I've figured it out just a little bit

Is it the measure of strength you might force
yourself to have when it'd be easier to succumb to
weakness?
Or is it perseverance when giving up seems to be
the best option?
Is it finding just a slither of light to hold onto
when the situation seems the darkest?

I'd like to think it's a combination of all three
All those things you've become for me
And everything I wish to be for you
I used to THINK I knew what Love was
Now I know for sure it's our glue

e. antoinette   137

You're so deep down in my system
It'd take rehab to rid me of you
Sometimes I have to refrain from speaking
As your name wants to come out even when it isn't
about you
I seem to be intoxicated by your love
Caught up in the rapture of this drug
And every time I think the feeling is gone
A memory reminds me that it'll never be too long
To be without you or hear from you or just to look
upon your face
You're more than you, you're a part of me
And that part can never be replaced

When I'm with you nothing else matters
I'm my happiest
And my thoughts are no longer scattered

You're a breath of fresh air
And a taste of freedom
You turn my dreams into reality
And you make me a believer

Things deemed impossible
You handle with ease
I'm inspired to be better
Because of your example

I can tune the world out
In your presence
You've captured my heart
When I'm with you
I'm on the ultimate high
And nothing else matters

I want to run away…. with you
To another time and place
Where things make more sense
Or even no sense at all but all was well
And all was peaceful
And the only thing that mattered was the way
lovers looked into each other's eyes,
Held hands walking in the path of the moonlight
And spoke only of the happiness and joy simplicity
brings

Instead, I'm forced to enjoy you over morning
chatter and evening traffic jams
News of wartime and constant collateral damage
Stories of despair and fights everywhere

I want to run away…with you
To another time and place
And can only long for the moments that we can
pretend to escape

If wishes could come true
And I had only one,
Regardless of everything else I want in life,
I'd use it on you.

I'll Follow Where You Lead

I'd follow you til the ends of the earth

Where the sky meets the ocean
And no lines are drawn

Where the depths of the waters
Go on for meters

Where the rainbow starts
With an undiscoverable ending

Til the ends of the earth
I'll follow where you lead me

Tried to Write a Love Song

I'm filled with a myriad of poems for you
Of love ballads and slow songs
And poetic lyrics I have yet to say.

I'm filled with the rhythm and the blues
And the soul of artists from our parents' time
People like Smokey Robinson and Marvin Gaye.

And sometimes I put these words to tunes
And sing em aloud, hoping you'll hear em
And regard em something like lullabies.

So overcome with admiration
I got enough love inside to write decades more
songs
About you and I.

I Can't Sleep Part VI

I went to sleep after I talked to you.

You made me laugh
When all I wanted to do was cry

I wanted to give up
And I thought of you
Hearing your voice interrupt my solitude
I'd been caught up in fairy tales and make-believe
And you brought me back to reality
Where life Can be a bed of ease
But only if and when you chose
to create such a thing
for yourself with no dependency
And you alone pick the things to which you wish to
cling

And sleep came to my eyes
As if I'd never rested before
There was no hesitance
Only content as I did not enter a dream world
Nor a state of oblivion
But I'd arrived at peace

A place of rest...

..and it was like taking my first breath.

PHILAUTIA
SELF-LOVE
(Loving Oneself)

I owe my heart an apology
for thinking it was as strong as my mind.

And I owe my mind an apology
for trusting it to handle matters of my heart.

Ascension

You chose to douse the flame
I lay in the ashes and rested in the embers
Until my Ascension, like a Phoenix
Ablaze and renewed, my fire burns with new
energy

All for you to try and return and enjoy the warmth
Just to find you could no longer lay claim to any
part of this hearth

Daydreaming

I'm all alone in a cold solitary place
No one can hear me or see the chilling look upon
my face
I'm not longing for attention or hoping for an
embrace
Just because I don't talk to you doesn't mean I am
displaced
Dark corridors and walls surrounding
There's no Prince Charming crouched down on
one knee
Not a good dream to you it may seem
All the darkness, no lighting or gleam
But look deeper into the enveloping darkness
Don't be stubborn but harken
For there lies something gracious
Above and beyond all not to be mistaken for
shapeless
Like an angel it guards and like a mist it lingers
Don't be afraid, reach for its fingers
Its warm interior and comfortable hold
What is this beautiful creature?
Please wait, and let it unfold
It slowly opens its eyes for the very first time
Beholding this wretched place watching all the sin
and crimes
Its thoughts say *I don't need this I'd rather have peace*
But I say *I need you to come and hold me in this cold
solitary place*
Erase the chilling look off my face
It smiles and answers *For you my child, living in this
pit, to rescue you, will be worthwhile*
So I become content and begin to shine
This heartfelt spirit has just become mine

Then I wake up startled and shudder all over
What a beautiful daydream I have just uncovered
But later on I realize I'm safe and free
Seems as though my spirit did come and rescue me

The Road is My Sanctuary

When everything is crashing around me
And falling behind me
I know I can always look ahead
Look for what's to come
At the beauty of what's before me
At the splendor of nature
As I travel the rugged terrain of life
Rather leaving or coming back
Traveling the same path or a brand new one
The calm of the ride is therapy
My mind, my heart, soul, and spirit
For once all aligned
In silence or disarray
No feeling can compare to having union of mind,
body, and soul
All while experiencing the splendor of nature
With the windows rolled down
Sun blocked by shade, hair in the wind
Or rain hitting my face
The thought of the destination is what keeps me
Music blasting drown my thoughts
As I grin about what lies ahead
Picturing whatever's next
Knowing no matter what it is, the trip would've
been worth it
For sanity's purpose
Enjoying the scenery that is the splendor of nature
Riding the curves of the mountains is my favorite
It's like my body, the vehicle and the road all join
in sync
And the trees watch the rhythm of the flow
I blast my music louder and now I'm riding the
beat

And if it's night the sky seems to throw the stars
right at me
The Big and Little Dipper dance with the North
Star
And my smile matches their brightness
In the dark, they can see my teeth
And the ride is more exciting, enjoying the
splendor of nature
In those moments I am the closest to God
And can hear Him the clearest
Forgiving me of my past and wiping my tears
Promising me a greater future, opened doors and
love everlasting
I look at the clouds, how they look like the ocean
Examine the trees, how a few rides ago all the
leaves were gone
And now they're showing
I cross bridges that stand over the most beautiful
bodies of water
I watch the mist how it rises and lingers especially
early morning
Sunrises and sunsets are my favorite
It reminds me of a lifetime, of things I have yet to
explore
The road is my sanctuary and
My God! The splendor of nature

Mountain Glory

Reality used to be beautiful
A dream of epic proportions
Plans for the future and goodbye to the past
My vision was clear no sign of distortion
Heart content and soul festive
Nighttime was the brightest
Dangers seen and unseen
Yet his arms protective
Perfection I'd reach and the sight was glorious
Escaping all battles together we were victorious
I decided to take a walk in the shadows
To ponder on what I might've been missing
Stepped down into the valley for the sole purpose
of reminiscing
I found myself being swallowed up and almost
drowned in sorrow
The earth quaked tremendously, and I could only
wish for the morrow
I began to sink and was frightened at the thought
that I'd diminish
All I could say was
"But I'm not finished"
The harder I fought to pull myself out of the pit
I realized my ascension, my fight, my will and
desire not to quit
The strength I found I 'thought' I had in you
But after hitting rock bottom I gained a totally
different view
Reality is no longer beautiful, my dreams no longer
epic
Sight isn't the clearest and the past and the future
are no longer separate
Perfection, I know of none and it's ceased to exist

I've replaced naivety with wisdom and a little
acceptance to assist
Life's no bed of ease
No long-lasting contentment
It's a place where broken promises are the results
of such said commitment
But after the rode traveled and a lesson learned
I made it through without you a champion
And my victory is well earned

If only there was a woman like the night sky
Who shined as bright as the farthest star but still
caught your eye
If the depth of her stretched to the Earths end
But never ended because you could feel her within
If her virtue amazed you like a blue moon
And left you captivated because it left too soon

If there was a woman like the night sky
I promise I'd stare up at her forever
Engulfed by her noiseless vibrations
Intrigued by her beauty quite like misinterpreted
constellations
Many knowing of her name
But never understanding her purpose
Scholars tried to break down their meaning
Created fables all misleading
Tried to read the stars but never succeeded
That's that woman, my night sky
How I long to touch and understand
But am only pleasured by the eye
And so, my mind
Can only wonder and make-believe
That I'm seeing what I see
And even though I can't reach her, she's all over
me...

And when the moon is full but steadily fading away
That's when I love it the most
Reminding me of her curves
And how I love to watch her sway
Reminding me how I love to look up and gaze
At the night sky...

If only there was a woman...
I'd find her and keep her
I'd nourish her halves and illuminate her fulls

Be her sun shining through
Her celestial playground
For her fiery desires
I'd let her rest in the comfort of knowing her
truths
Help her withstand the times she felt she was
expiring
You know, when days begin and nights end
Reassuring her that she'd Always come again...

If only there was a woman...

The Cost of Perfection

I've come to learn that searching for perfection is more detrimental than accepting reality. On the quest to no mistakes, no issues or problems...or rather no flaws, one may mistakenly create a bigger...flaw...for lack of a better word, than what was begun with. One can strive so hard to alter reality that everyday situations are almost overlooked, to the point that one always thinks futuristic-ally but not in the present...that which exists now.

The danger of the quest for perfection is destruction. In the attempt of reaching a dream/vision of perfection, one can unknowingly kill those surrounding them (i.e. friendships, spirits, etc.) As seen on both an emotional and physical level there is no possible way of reaching perfection. We can aim for excellence, but the search for perfection almost always leads to anything besides that...perhaps another headache...or sleepless night...

Gain Content.

Be Happy for the Imperfections, for Perfection COSTS more.

She Is LOVE, and that's why it flows so freely.
She Gives LOVE, even if others take so frivolously.

She Is PATIENCE, and so she endures the hands
of time.
She Gives PATIENCE, to those who feel left
behind.

She Is HOPE, and that why she keeps the faith.
She Lives HOPEFUL, not to be confused with
anxiety to pass today.

She Is STRENGTH, and that's why others cling to
her tightly.
She Gives STRENGTH, even though weakness
tries to slide in ever so slightly.

She Is ALL of us and who We aspire to be.
She Is Her and I am SHE.

Queen

She wears pain like a badge of honor
Hope is her sword
Faith is her strength
Her smile lights up in the darkest of hours
Replacing the grim truths of her reality
With her head held high
She faces the world as if she's never been defeated
And unconquerable becomes her
Her thrown awaiting her to be seated.

The Rose that Grew from Concrete

Did you hear about the rose that grew from the
concrete?
Proving nature's law is wrong, it learned to walk
without having feet.
Funny, it seems, by keeping its dreams, it learned
to breathe fresh air.
Long live the rose that grew from the concrete,
when no one else ever cared....

    -   *Tupac Shakur*

.... ever cared to share or heal or reveal to the rose
its true purpose.
The rose though never plucked and replaced, but
also not shown its virtue.
Or the amount of what lied within it, what it truly
deserved or the depth of its value.
Inhabitants surrounding it, desiring to keep it
hidden in the shadows.
But the rose grew from the concrete anyway.
Proving nature's law is wrong, it learned how to
make it out its own way.

    -   *Elizabeth Antoinette*

The End.

Questions and Answers with the Author

Q: Is this book about one person?
A: This book is not about every person I've dated, but rather people who've driven me to write. Some pieces are factual, while others are fiction – with a little exaggeration in both... The oldest poem in this book is 16 years old, so that should tell you a lot.

Q: Do you really suffer insomnia?
A: There have been several periods in my life that I thought I was experiencing insomnia. It wasn't until I got a regular 8 to 5 that I considered maybe I just had poor sleeping habits transitioning out of college into adulthood, LOL. Nevertheless, I have experienced nights that my thoughts plagued me so deeply that I could not find rest. Occasionally, on some of those nights, one of the means of finding sleep was to write. Coincidentally, the series of poems entitled *I Can't Sleep* began, and led to the creation of this book.

Q: Why did you feel the need for "A Summary of Sorts"?
A: Upon first completing this book, or rather thinking that I'd completed it, I attempted to read it as if I hadn't written it and immediately became confused. So, I decided to explain the making of the book and define the sections and subsections for the comprehension of all readers. Readers may start the book off without reading *"A Summary of Sorts"* and refer to it later for a clearer understanding of the flow of the book.

Q: Are there multiple interpretations for each of your pieces or just one assigned to each?
A: For most of the pieces there is an exact feeling or interpretation assigned, however, I like to leave anything I write to the interpretation of the reader. It always amazes me to hear the thoughts of my readers and the things that came to their mind while reading; sometimes, so much so, to the point, I wonder what was going through my subconscious while writing.

Q: What is your favorite part about writing?
A: My favorite part about the writing process is reading a piece in its entirety immediately after writing it. I get so excited! and immediately begin thanking God for this talent He's given me. I absolutely love the imagery and the imagination that I write with. It still amazes me, as if I was reading another author's pieces.

Q: What do you want your readers to take away from this book?
A: I want them to enjoy thinking of themselves and their past, present, future and potential relationships. I want them to relate to each section and realize that they're not the only one in the world experiencing the complication that is love. It can be one of the most beautiful feelings and turn around and become one of the most agonizing too, but whatever it is to you, enjoy the actual moment and realize that nothing lasts forever, good or bad.

*Q: **Will all your future books be series of poems?***

A: No. As this is my first published book, I wanted it to be introductory for me as an author, but not to define me as writer. My goal is to write non-fiction, fiction, and biographical pieces. I have considered a sequel to this book, but futuristically, I want to create a library of different genres.

Acknowledgments

Lord, I thank You for this talent you've given me.
It still leaves me in awe and amazement every time
I'm blessed with the ability to complete a piece and
sit in wonder that the words on the paper have
come from me. You said in Your word that a man's
gift makes room for him (Proverbs 18:16 NKJV)
and admonished us to use our gifts to serve one
another (1 Peter 4: 10 ESV). I thank You for giving
me the boldness and confidence to share my gift
with others in hopes that my story may help
someone make it through theirs.

I must thank my immediate family, mama
(Shadonna), Seria, David, and Shaina. You all know
I love you with everything in me. I cherish the
strength of our family no matter what challenges
life throw at us. With every goal I
complete there's an ultimate sense of
accomplishment for US. To Sontidra, keep fighting
on. I love you (and yours) for life.

I must also thank my extended family (BBL!),
friends, principals, teachers, administrators,
schoolmates, colleagues, neighbors, coaches,
pastors, ministers, fellow church members,
supervisors, co-workers, etc., who've turned into
family members - for your contributions in my
circle of influence. There are so many of you, in
different times and places, in many ways, who've
helped to shape me into the woman I am thus far.
So as not to leave anyone off this list, I've included
specific locations and time periods. Just know, even
if your name isn't mentioned, my memory won't let

me forget the impact of those significant periods in my life, and I thank you for whatever role you may have played on your stop of my journey. With that being said, here's to:

The Binghampton Community, forever and always, Memphis, TN; Lester Elementary School, 1993-2001, Memphis, TN; Creative Learning in a Unique Environment (C. L. U. E.), 1996- 2003, Memphis, TN; Zoe Ministries International, 1998-2010, Memphis, TN; East High School (including all the many extracurricular activities I took part in lol), 2001-2007, Memphis, TN; Teen Appeal Memphis, 2004-2007, Memphis, TN; The University of Tennessee, Knoxville, 2007-2011, Knoxville, TN; My Little in Big Brother Big Sister of East Tennessee, 2009-2011, Knoxville, TN; DialAmerica Marketing, Inc, 2010-2012, Knoxville, TN; GC Services, LP, Student Loan Division, 2013-2018, Knoxville, TN; UT Event Staff (Football & Basketball), Sammie Henderson's Team, 2016-2018, Knoxville, TN. Thank all y'all, love y'all!

I would be remiss to not praise the editor of the first draft of this book, my eighth-grade literature teacher, Mrs. Toni Lester, from whom I stole the coined phrase, "Care? Fresh out." Thank you so much, for your gestures of kindness back then and for not hesitating when I asked you to do this for me.

Last, but not least, I can not fail to thank the geniuses involved with making my vision of this cover come to life: first, with his precision in photography, Daryl Johnson of Astute

Photography (www.astutelenz.com), second, my hairstylist, Tish Flye (www.foreverflye.com) and makeup artist, Brooke Foust (www.brooklynbeatface.com) and last, my friend Justin Walker (The BlaQ Knight); for their contributions toward the photo shoot and the final edits on the cover. Thank you all for helping me put the last piece of the puzzle together, to add the icing to the cake.

Meet the Author

Elizabeth Antoinette Ross was born and raised in the great city of Memphis, TN. The eldest of 4 to Shadonna Becton-Ross (Philadelphia, PA), Elizabeth prides herself on being a great friend and is family-oriented. She is honored to be a Memphian, but refers to herself as a Tennessean, as she currently resides in Knoxville, TN, the home to her Alma Mater, THE University of Tennessee, Knoxville. At UT Knoxville, Elizabeth obtained a Bachelor of Arts in English and Technical Communication. She later obtained her Master of Business Administration from King University, Bristol, TN.

Elizabeth began reading at the tender age of 2 years old. Her mother reminds her all the time of her desire to read at that age, so much so, that Elizabeth would cry when she saw her older half-siblings reading and would whine, *"I want to read too."*

Elizabeth's love for literacy, translated into her excelling and exceeding educational requirements as a scholar throughout school, even as much as skipping the second grade and participating in off-campus studies in a program for gifted children called C.L.U.E. (Creative Learning in a Unique Environment) from primary to secondary school.

Her first publication was at the age of 6, in Memphis' Commercial Appeal, a comic-drawn picture, captioned, *"Playing with My Friends."* Elizabeth went on to write for multiple newspaper publications including, The Teen Appeal (Memphis, TN), The Daily Beacon (The University of Tennessee, Knoxville, TN) and the Knoxville News Sentinel (Knoxville, TN). However, Elizabeth's passion has always been in storytelling and creative writing. Having no desire to follow rules of expression or for writing, she decided to forego writing for news and fulfill her goal of becoming a published author.

Elizabeth is currently the owner and operator of The Director of Creativity, LLC, an organization dedicated to fostering creative branding and consulting in the form of literature, with emphasis on editing and publishing. She can be contacted for her services at thedirectorofcreativity.com. She also publishes poems and short stories on her Instagram page @elizabeth.antoinette.